POST & LINE

POST & LINE

POEMS

ANNE DAMROSCH

Wild Rising Press

EVERGREEN, COLORADO

Book Design: Mary M. Meade
Editor: Judyth Hill
First Edition
ISBN 978-1-957468-40-2

For my family

Contents

❧

LINES

POSTS

Pages 39–42

❧

LINES

FIVE PROSE PIECES

I

II

III

IV

V

LINES

Hanging Laundry

Between contractions,
my second birth, a girl born forty years ago,
I read *Travels With Charley*,
studied a photography book of laundry lines
strung up across America in the fifties or sixties,
slung between backyard trees, flown
like semaphores, porch roof to side of barn,
or pulleyed window to window
above a back alley in a New York City slum.
In my altered state
it was easy to see them as the art form they were,
a statement of female identity you could say—
family portrait pinned-up, sock by sock,
and sent off into the sunny day,
flapping shirts and billowing overalls,
an alternate, cleaned-up version of the family,
while the real one was off at the factory, at school,
or napping in a crib upstairs.
Where did she place herself?
Next to her man? Last in line?
Farthest away from him?
Flanked by her children?
My kids don't have laundry lines.
You can hear my son's family dryer
sounding its efficient rhythms all through the house.
It's my son-in-law's job to load a bag
bulging with the week's laundry into a metal cart,
rattle it down the street to the wash-and-fold on Flatbush.
My daughter is pregnant with baby number four.

Everyone says she's brave or crazy.
She is neither and both.
I don't remember a thing about Steinbeck's road trip,
except Charley was a poodle,
and the truck was called *Rocinante*.
I wonder how many of those backyard trees are still alive,
towering over the towns of darkened mills and rusted tracks.
I still hang my laundry up. It lightens my footprint,
and I like how it makes my towels feel,
a little bit scratchy and stiff,
smelling of some sweet mix of molecules,
soap and water, and oxygen freshly exhaled
from the apple tree and cedar hedge.
I like how my pants and shirts wave and bow in the breeze.
I have time to dabble in different art forms now.
It's good when my clothes all fit on one line.
A poem on one page.

Nesting Season

Disasters are myriad:

>Bluejay attack,
>hatchling snatched.

>Six phoebes wither
>while the cowbird grows fat.

>After a week of late spring snow
>the nuthatch pair abandons their nest.

>They cover the eggs with their own feather down
>before they go.

Flying lessons are risky too:

>Rocky landings, ill-fated falls,
>raccoons prowl, crows patrol.

Still, most nests empty as designed:

>The family soars,
>swelling the flock,
>and the vacant nest, a tidy cup
>lined with moss and milkweed silk,
>starts to tatter.

On this first warm day of April
after an arctic winter

my city strides out whistling and humming.
We walk our dogs and babies to the park.

We ride our bikes to work,
with rolled-up blueprints tucked under our arms.

We choose our sites,
enumerate the obstacles and enemies.

Such bravery swells my heart—
despite reports of advancing fire and flood,

this risky thing
of assembling something beautiful.

Front Page, *New York Times*

It isn't meant to be beautiful,
this image of a red car
sinking into the rising
New Jersey floodwater,

but the water
is blue and glassy
and the red car,
so silent.

I am sorry
if this is your car,
or the car of your friend,
or if it reminds you of the car you drove
during your second year of college,
named after a girl,
Jenny or Stella.

You could say
the car in the newspaper
is dying.
It will never again thrum and roar
down the entrance ramp to the New Jersey Turnpike,
nor fight for a parking space
at the Vince Lombardi rest stop.

It is simply
a red island
in a small lake,

resplendent,
grand,
azure water rising and spreading around it
like a gown.

Spider Silk Weaving at the
Museum of Natural History

This is what the fourth king wanted to bring,
this wondrous cloth woven of gold,
for thousands of years an alchemist's dream.
It lies smooth, stretched-out and sealed
inside an eleven-foot-long glass case,
glowing as if its threads were spun
from the pure light of a late fall afternoon,
as if it would disappear
if you could only touch it.

You make your journey,
braving no more than a missed flight and a lost suitcase,
riding packed subways on a Saturday afternoon,
and walk through the frozen park
to the long flight of steps up to the museum doors.
Inside the bustling lobby, shedding backpack and coat,
you pay your money and follow your map,
past the glazed tourists sitting in the shade of dinosaur bones.

What have they come to see?
The universe displayed and explained?
Real butterflies in their hair?

It really isn't so strange no one stops
before a tapestry in a box—
how would they know to read the label
that says there's a miracle in their midst?

Someone needs to tell the story—
how in the highlands of Madagascar
seventy men and women snared golden orb spiders with
    long poles
through four rainy seasons, a million female spiders,
as big as your hand.
They only bit if the people moved too fast,
but would devour each other
if not placed each in her own box.

Who would believe such a strange story?

how the women placed the spiders in harnesses,
in rows of twenty three,
extracting a single strand of silk from the stilled body,
a thread as fine as a child's hair,
which in four years
never once broke—

how still
no one understands
the way fluid inside the spider's body
is transformed into gossamer
the second it emerges into air.

You want to see the hands
that twisted the silk into one thread
soft and supple,
but stronger than steel wire.

You want to know if it was the hand
or the motor that turned the reel,

and if the women sang and talked to the spiders
or only told their troubles to each other.

You imagine the quiet
at the end of the long day,
after all the years of spinning were over,
the shelves stacked with golden spools
awaiting the weavers,
awaiting the loom.

And the empty boxes,
the spiders released.

You know there's a key somewhere
to let you open this case,
roll up the cloth, hide it inside your coat
and carry it safely out into the world.

You want to take it home,
back to the hands that made it.
They will lay it out on the ground
to receive the weaver's baby.

Deft brown hands will swaddle him in gold
and sling a shining hammock between two trees,
rocked by the wind
under the orbs
where the spiders
are silently spinning.

Henry's Garden

I peer over the fence to see if there's something new.
Just when it seems there's no room for another thing,
a soda bottle birdhouse appears, dangling from an eave,
though I wonder what bird would build in this neighborhood,
patrolled nightly by raccoons, tabbies and rats.
This garden is made for the eyes.
Its winding path, edged with every-other-inverted glass beer
    bottles,
is too narrow for human feet to walk with ease,
especially Henry, who I know to be a big man.

I see him looking out from his chair by the window
at his favorite time of the day,
when the fork and spoon wind chimes are silent,
and the late afternoon sunshine sparkles off the tines.
A vintage hubcap stills from twirling in the garden's solitary tree,
and marigolds busting out of their dented bucket are aglow.

Henry's gaze takes a walk around the broken-slate jigsaw-puzzle
    path
and stops to linger on a rampant tomato vine
that has engulfed its wire cage propped up by a ski pole,
and the sweet peas that twine over the crisscrossing strings
of their broom-and-sponge-mop tipi.

I think he must know how beautiful are
these things he has given a second life.
Today he's revised the garden at its very center,

laid a tidy wall of angled half-bricks in a circle around his Mary,
raised her up on a cinderblock plinth,
so now the light can reach the top of her head.

Henry must be a morning gardener like me—
I've never seen him at it,
only traces of his inner landscapes,
dream-tailings and evidence of the joy
of his hands at play in his own square of earth.

Inside the sweet limits of a picket fence
cloaked in morning glories, this afternoon
the closing flowers give a last glimpse
of the most honest blue
beyond the sky.

Before Blue

Long before painters cloaked a virgin in blue,
before Mohammed, wearing green, on his milk-white steed,
before India extracted indigo from a shrubby pink-flowered
    bean,
or Afghanis ground their lapis stones into ultramarine,
before Egypt smelted cobalt from arsenic-laden goblin ore,
before people invented things blue, and attached names to
    them—

    no blue.
    The theory:
    the ancients didn't see blue
    before they had a name for it.

Which is to say no one noticed
the bandwidth between violet and green.

Could it be
some kind of hunger or greed,
desire to possess, commodify and keep,
begets the giving of names?
Hard not to imagine barefoot women of yore,
sun-kissed naked toddlers tied on their backs,
scooping water, carrying it home on their heads down a rocky
    path.
Did that pure desert blue above them lighten their load?
Did they watch with wonder as the full moon rose over a calm
    azure sea,
or only gaze, into Homer's wine-dark depths?

Ulysses, like you and me, couldn't love
what he couldn't see.
Wine, his only solace as he languished
so far from his lover Penelope,
the sea beneath his decks
deep and dark and full of fear.
And though the *rosy-fingered dawn*
greeted him with hope renewed,
neither his sky nor his lover were clothed in blue.
That kind of name-laden treasuring
requires the promise of things we can hold.

To own is a dream of enlarging
our frightened, hungry selves.
But to stand alone under infinite radiance,
nothing between you and unnamable mystery—
no name, no need, no time, no you.

Fireworks

We stroll along the bike path to the beach.
My granddaughters spill their soda
and squabble on the cramped blanket.
The grownups' wine tastes of bug spray.
No one on our blanket
is thinking about Thomas Jefferson or the Continental Congress,

or the chemical composition of the rockets,
whether it's strontium or lithium that makes the red glare,
sodium or barium for the blue,
or the labels on the sawdust-filled boxes from China
that read like haiku,

Bengal fire, Peony, Horsetail, Falling Leaf.
No one is thinking about the US/China trade imbalance,
    because
this may be the best civilization has to offer,

its citizens seated on beach towels waiting for darkness to fall,
bare feet stuck out in front of them,
their children splashing in the small waves,
throwing sticks for rescue dogs.

The first tentative launch is followed quickly
by more blunted thunder,
silent avalanches of flowering embers.
The dogs tremble and strain at their leashes.

We raise our faces, and breathe our collective *ohs* and *ahs*.
This is what we have come for,

this miniaturized and domesticated fire power,
silver rain falling harmlessly on water.

And later, back at home, after the moon has come up,
the open windows let in the lingering scent of smoke.
You can still catch a whiff of it
after everyone has gone to bed.

Blood Moon

After the drought, after the blood moon,
the rains came, and stayed for three days

like a long lost uncle, who shows up for the holiday meal
with a nice bottle of wine, stays to wash the dishes,
sleep uncomplaining on the couch
and in the morning, sweep the floor.

The all-night all-day rain refilled gravel streambeds,
scoured away scorched leaves,
twiggy bones of desiccated frogs.
It was a kind and beneficent rain that soaked
through the brittle sod,
replenishing root, aquifer and spring.

When the sky cleared
everything shone, and was good again.
Sidewalks and blackbirds reflected rainbows.
Rinsed stones rekindled their colors.

Summer ended on that day
and the trees turned up their flames.
But nobody remembers those rains.
We forget about weather.

And the blood moon?
TV prophets foretold it. All flesh
would see it together, from where we sat
out on our front porches, fire escapes and decks,
beside the gas grill, pool toys and frisbees,
saw it framed in airplane windows, and tent flaps tied back

to reveal the moon's face rising over the desert,
over a mishmash patchwork of rooftops
fashioned of plastic and metal and thatch,
where the sky was a black velvet backdrop
for the moon's ruddy face.

Maybe you cupped your hands against a square of safety glass
twenty stories up over a never-dark city.
Someone remembers a moon
that kept the elephants awake, jostling the trees,
and no one slept that night,
in the ICU, or the prison.

In spite of the fluorescent lights' glare, someone remembers
the full-on face of the moon leaning in,
saw the blood and rust shadow of us seeping across,
the body of our own body traveling through.

Another Poem About the Moon

Between the stacks of gray brick buildings
I catch a glimpse of the moon in pieces,
glinting between the dry leaves of a sycamore.

The moon seems supernaturally bright,
undimmed by haze and the sick glow of sodium vapor lights.
It startles me. It seems the only real thing around,

still here, stripped of myth,
just a rock, sort of a she,
carrying her own rhythms, while I've lost track.

I don't know if she's a slender crescent
because she's young or old.
For now, it matters only that I see

her existence depends upon my gaze:

> The sensory apparatus clicks on.
> Somewhere in the parietal lobe
> a bundle of cells lights up,
> selects the crescent shape from the surround,
> projects its miniaturized image upside down
> on the screen behind my eyes.
> Then neatly reverses it.
> Voila! The moon produced
> and named: crescent, not gibbous.
> Waxing or waning? I don't know.

The eyes could move on to other things,
or they could stay and see
that the moon is a sturdy life raft,

keeping a steadfast and safe distance
from the mothership.
Beyond her, the infinite unknowable,

and both of us, barely rescued from impossibility.

I promise I'll keep better track,
do better by the moon,
the way the rivers and tides of my body,

unperceived like air, have been doing all along.
Of course, the moon needs nothing from me,
certainly not another poem. But speaking of need,

it's not hard to imagine endless nothingness
with no intermediary to translate between light and dark,
no mirror in the night to assure us

our star still shines,
no stepping stone
where we might pause and rest before we leap.

Shostakovich String Quartet No. 8, Dedicated to the Victims of War and Fascism

We should never have sat in the front row.

We were like voyeurs at an accident scene,
unable to turn away
from the terrible cries of the wounded.
One moment the bows flayed the strings,
the next, slowly extracted glass shards
from the disembodied memories
of the missing.

The musicians' faces flinched
as they gave voice to what they saw before their eyes,
so strangely encoded.

The Eighth could have been a suicide note
or its cathartic substitute,
vehicle for blunt survival.
Perhaps there was some solace in knowing
it will be impossible now
for us to forget what we have heard.

Is this why we make things?
The old sounds cannot hold
this life. We grope in the dark
for other vessels.
Our pens are empty.

Imagine a time when our tools were made of stone,
when we worked under the naked sky
in the presence of fire.

What did we remember?
How did we remember?
How did we grieve
before there were names for the ones
missing around the fire?

How did we live through a season
when the earth was scorched and bare
and yielded no fruit?
Before there was a word to call up the sound
and the smell of rain.
Was there music?
How did we hope?

One Year to Live

for Stephen Levine

One Year To Live is actually a place,
a small village rimmed by snow-covered mountains.
It is where you live and know
you will never live anywhere else.
It is where you are awakened before dawn by a barking dog,
and your fearful demons
parade before you in their latest disguises.
So you take a book from a shelf by your bed
and begin to read words you have read before.
Later in the morning you will put on a sweater
and go out to buy your breakfast.
And though the store has run out of oranges and there's no
    raisin bread,
you know you won't be going elsewhere to look
for what you thought you wanted to eat.
You will take your bag of apples and plain bread
and walk to the pond in the park
with its pairs of ducks and geese and one swan.
You will sit down on a bench to eat the apples and the bread.
But instead you will jump up
and help two boys find their dog who has run away.
And after the three of you have caught the dog, you will discover
the pigeons have found your bread,
and a huge flock is gathering from all parts of the earth,
sailing in on outstretched wings in the cool morning air,
a wild flurry of dappled gray feathers, spotted and streaked,
white and black, lavender, blue.
The iridescent feathers around their necks are glowing opals.

They land like angels on pink feet and stride about
in patches of sunshine and shade,
cooing to themselves and to each other.
They are so happy to be here eating the bread.
And when the sparrows come down from the trees
to sweep up the last tiny crumbs,
you see everything is here,
all of it,
right here.

On That Day

On that day, the blue tipped matches will rest side by side
in their sandpapered box,

beside the slender incense sticks,
and the unstruck bell.

On that day, the keys, the hat, and the blue sweater,
worn thin at the elbows, will hang on their hooks,

and the sturdy vacuum cleaner, its cord coiled tight,
will not begin to hum at the touch of my foot

nor huff across the rug,
knocking at table legs.

The forks and spoons will nest in their slotted drawer.
The silent pencils will stand up in their jar,

next to the scissors
pointed down.

On that day, the crabgrass and weeds by the front door
will continue to crowd the stones of the path,

and the colonies of red and black ants underground
will lay a few thousand new eggs, perfect and smooth as grains
    of rice.

On that day, no automatic door
will open at the sight of me.

On that plain and ordinary day,
the feather-down pillow my head has pressed

will inhale and regain its form,
full and rounded as a snow mound,

as it has always done.
Just as all the things of the world will continue

to know how to do and be,

on that very day,
that last day,

when the animal I am
will know what to do,

how to let go of being me.

Dear Catherine,

Was it you who placed your wedding photo on the baby grand?
I wonder when you last touched those keys.

Could you hear the Bach cantatas we played for you?
Taizé songs from the speaker by your ear? Did you hear the loons?

In the long pauses between your breaths,
could you hear the music better? Were you practicing your rests?

Did you hear the hospice nurse ask about your favorite drink?
I hope you tasted the fuzzy navel Owen made to moisten your
    mouth.

Did you hear him say? "We're here, it's safe for you to go."
Was it true? I know you would give me the truth if you could.

Did you feel the small, warm body of your favorite kitty,
    Guinevere,
pressed against your hip?

Maybe you could catch the whiff of mud and salt in the air,
drifting up from the river. Did you hear the rain on the roof?

Could you smell the coffee pot refilling
as friends who love you came by?

You didn't need to know I got lost driving to the store,
and passed the same dead skunk twice,

nor how, miles from where you lay, I dropped a bottle of red wine
in the beverage aisle at Lee's Market,

and a young man appeared with a mop and bucket, a new bottle,
and forgiveness. How the store was full of angels,

and in that moment, it was possible to know
all beings to be of equal value. Thanks to you. Thank you.

And at home, while you breathed, and practiced your measured
  pauses,
the soundtrack of life continued around you,

beer cans popping,
family stories and laughter in the kitchen,

onions sizzled in a black iron skillet, and in a big red pot,
codfish chowder simmered on the back of the stove.

The next morning the house was quiet.
In a little sagging hollow, in the middle of your empty bed,

your Guinevere was curled up asleep, keeping your place warm.
I just wanted you to know.

At His Cousin's Funeral My Ex-Husband Wears a Red Bow Tie

What has happened to you?
Quirky tinkerer,
half boy/half bird.
What kind? Bowerbird,
builder of intricate never-finished nests,
devotee of honeybees and the golden mean,
the Tao, and any old thing with wheels.

Here you are with your new wife, a harpist,
singing a duet.
She beams up at you,
adores this current version of you.

I don't mourn.
I did my grieving long ago,
incrementally, particle by particle
we lost our ease.
No way to try at freedom and flow,
the most slippery of gifts,
like pretending to play.

But where did the boy go?
And the girl who loved him?
And just who is this inside a crisp white shirt
bedecked with a red bow tie? Wherefore the bow tie?

The funeral was billed as a celebration of Catherine's life—
maybe, the tie was meant to be festive, and now it's all wrong,
as you read a four-page treatise in dead earnest,

your version of another's life to tell,
as if it were the truth.

Where is the one who half-knew
the elusiveness of truth?
Did you follow the wrong instructions?
The ones that said
To sever head from heart, cut here.
Maybe the tie was your wife's idea.
She wanted a capital C Catholic.
You tried, in your way,
but where did you stash all your pesky questions?
Orthodoxy never suited your Sagittarian mind.

Outside the window of the Quaker meeting house
I spot a figure, an old man partially hidden in a grove of pines.
When the wind lifts a branch
I see him sitting on a wobbly stool.
It's Lao Tzu, in his ragged shirt/baggy pants disguise.
He's been here all along, listening in to my monkey mind,
chuckling to himself.

Around his neck a red thread of blessing.
The joke's on me, but he still loves me,
and you, and the red bow tie.

Reading *A Child's Christmas in Wales*

It is evening.
Three generations sit down in a living room
littered with the flotsam of Christmas day.
This year there's a new baby
and a newly divorced neighbor,
her first Christmas alone.

I extract a half-eaten candy cane
wedged between two couch pillows
before I take my place next to the eight-year-old.

Last year she couldn't have navigated *Hop on Pop*.
Now she sails through the first page of the story,
including the lines:
I could never remember whether it snowed for six days and six nights when
I was twelve or whether it snowed for twelve days and twelve nights when I
was six.
She is as untroubled by the skimpy punctuation
and quirky syntax
as the next reader, her dentist grandfather, is troubled by it.

The Welshman's words are passed hand to hand around the room,
now intoned with a thick South Boston accent,
now in a voice muddled by wine and riches,
and by minds just struggling to take hold
of the strange meanderings of another man's mind.

I love this story,
and it doesn't matter at all what happens
because it is true

the words need us,
need us to form them again in our clumsy mouths,
swaddling them with our thick tongues
bringing them forth, words
that are but remnants of another man's memories
wondrously reimagined.

Murmured together,
they become our own memories.
It doesn't matter
that the words dissolve
the instant they're spoken,
like snowflakes falling on the Welsh sea.

The little red dog-eared book travels around the circle.
We read our treasured pages
as some of us have done
nearly every Christmas for forty years
in other rooms
now inhabited by strangers.

The last reader closes the book.
The room is silent for a few moments,
except for the overtones of other voices
sounding beyond our walls.

The neighbor wipes away a tear
and gets up to start on the dishes.
Someone pops a bottle,
the baby grows restless.
His mother wraps him in a blanket,
and walks him slowly around the room.

POSTS

11/9/16

6:30 AM the morning after Election Day
Judit calls from Montreal,
crying at her kitchen table.
The world is shrinking.
How will we go out?
Something is buzzing.
I have to put the phone down,
find a postcard and a cup,
to free a honeybee,
beating its wings against my windowpane.

11/10/16

Dear Emily,
when the apocalypse comes,
can I come live with you
on Amen Farm?

11/11/16

It's a good thing
the kingdom of the gods is within.
Outside isn't looking so good.

11/12/16

When you're awake
you're more in sync with your dog.
People are harder.

11/13/16

I make a collage.
The Quaker Oats man turns out to be a queen.
I haven't hung her up yet.
Queens can be shy,
now more than ever.

11/14/16

In Vermont some of us are popping a few too many
Heady Toppers.
You'll find us wandering the paths along the lake
looking for the supermoon rising,
looking for little acts of improvement—
sweep the floor, stack wood,
clean the basement.
We'll burn a huge pile
of brush and broken chairs
when the snow comes.

11/15/16

My son got serious about his war with the bluejays.
Now a flock of chickadees and finches
occupies the newly armored feeder,
above the grounded bully blues.

11/23/16

Who can write a poem about birds?
About Thanksgiving?

This is just to say,
please put the bird in the oven.
Take her out when her skin is brown
and her blood runs clear.

Let's just say I can't sleep past 4:00 AM.
Neither can the little Carolina wren outside my window
with a voice like Janis Joplin.

Freedom's just another word for nothin left to lose.

America's got too much to lose.
The dragon is burning
in her melting gold

11/26/16

The most useful advice I've heard was from the writers of
    Saturday Night Live—
Don't give up! It's Saturday night!
And that's right, because on Saturday night
you sit around with your family and your friends,
or you call them up and go out to see an alien invasion movie,
or stay home with your sweeties
and watch an alien invasion movie on Netflix,
cry when it turns out
the aliens just wanted to help us.
Play a game.
And when you go out to the kitchen to refill two wine glasses,
the kids are making their own s'mores on the stove burner.
It's a mess, but they promise to clean it up.
You tell them, hey,

everybody's doing a great job here.
And on Sunday morning,
you still remember that.

LINES

Goldfinches in Early Spring

I didn't see them
until I opened the door
and the whole flock rose up from the ground,
in their newly minted plumage
like fresh paint,
day-glow yellow,
as if all the yellow in the world—
butter cups and corn kernels,
daffodils, crocus pollen
carried on the legs of bumblebees,
handfuls of dandelions,
and in every child's first painting
the round sun
occupying an upper corner—
as if all the yellow,
all thought of yellow
were condensed in the bodies of these birds,
flying up into the dark branches
barely dotted with green,
little flames kindling in the branches,
warming us again,
the way light does always return,
sparks igniting one at a time and all at once,
new yellow leaves
miraculously returning to the trees,
reversing all together
the direction of fall.

Dog

the dog is rolling in the grass while I am mowing the lawn around him   he
just rolls and rolls and does an outrageously thorough job of it as if he wanted
to paint his whole black furry body the bright deep green of the grass and as I

move around the lawn   he keeps moving to
the places   where the   grass is lush and it
must feel so cool to a   dog   in fact   the grass is
longest   in the place   he's lying and I can't
make him move, he is   so old and I like the
sight of him lying there   inside the square of

long grass like a miniature dog–sized hayfield with one dandelion and one dog

The Old Dog Contemplates the Bardo

for Pippin

He may have already decided.
For fourteen years he's been watching me,
and there isn't much he doesn't get.
Sometimes, though, he cocks his head in puzzlement

as I outline some plan for the day.
To his credit, he's never fully mastered the future tense.
He reads my movements like a sailor at sea
smells the meaning of clouds,

how I rise with purpose on Mondays,
lie vagrant on Sunday mornings,
a day with its own comforting smells.
Yesterday at my computer an exasperated *tsk*

escaped my tongue,
made him rise from his post by the door,
and limp to my office dragging his back legs behind him,
just to see what was up.

Who knows?
It could be my life's best work
is to accompany my dog
on his way to becoming human.

The time is getting close.
He sleeps most of the day.
It may be up to me,
his yay or nay.

Some days I'm a poor advertisement for being human.

I may have command of the car keys,
cupboards and doors,
but not much else.

I neglect my pack, fuss over little things I lose.
He forgives
and forgives. But it worries him
when I get off balance.

When I remember
it's for both of us,
I try a little harder to go with the flow.
Of course, I learned that from him.

Now I need to let him know
about this being human,
whether or not
it's worth waking up for.

Swimmer

A young man,
so young, only one thought
under his baseball cap,
springs from his beat-up pickup truck, whistling
into the open mouths of his rubber waders,
anticipating the icy press
of stream on thighs,
ignites a cigar to foil the mosquitoes
and descends the moss-carpeted aisle,
an acolyte in an incense cloud
swinging rod and reel
into the deep
green cathedral shadows.

Under silent arches
a spark of cold fire strikes,
a jewel-studded fish,
eyes, gills, mouth agape,
gulping death and life simultaneously,
lies still for a moment in his hands
as if she trusts them to unhook,
then suddenly flips,
electric, alive,
slithers from his fingers
and disappears into the deep pool.

Years later
his newborn daughter,
trailing her cord like kelp,

slips into his open palms
and stays.
He gazes down
through salty pools.
Two deep, dark-blue fearless eyes
looking up
remember him.

Visitations

A pebble washes up from my dreams,
the image of a small owl I hold in my hand like a stuffed toy.
She is asleep. She is dying.
A tiny white mushroom, the size of a seed pearl,
grows from her third eye like a white bindi.
It has sickened her,
like the disease killing the bats.

She is the same owl who visited me fourteen years ago,
when I came home from work on a late fall afternoon,
sick with the flu.
Outside my bathroom window, in the dusky light,
I saw a small rounded shape in the viburnum bush
an arm's length from the glass.

A tiny owl, no bigger than a robin,
swiveled her head 180 degrees,
and aimed her eyes at me,
two perfect black circles ringed in gold,
a look not of fear, but youthful curiosity,
simply inquisitive and present.

Maybe her mother never taught her about humans.
She turned her head and surveyed the dark garden,
and then returned her gaze to look at me.
She let me turn the porch light on,
revealing the beauty of her stippled feathers,
in shades of warm brown, and pure white.
I took her picture before she flew,
forgot my wretched state for long elated minutes.

But my rational mind wouldn't allow me to believe
she came to comfort me.

I still don't
presume to know why she came.
But this morning she is back,
giving me a glimpse of her before she goes,
letting me thank her for her presence.

Woodchuck at Omega Institute

Nothing furtive about you.
In this place, where the practice is radical *ahimsa,*
even the mosquitoes are safe.

Your whole tribe
(think Krishna's peacocks, the Queen's corgis)
happily devouring the vegetable garden,
and at my feet, you, fattening yourself on clover.

Once I trapped a woodchuck
who was marauding my bean patch
(and anything else he liked) all day while I was at work.
When I got to him, the wire trap was littered with scat,
and from inside a scruffy old groundhog
bared his yellow teeth and chattered at me,
then let loose a horrible cry,
a quaking shriek of anguish and rage.

He froze in terror, silent as I wrapped him
and his stinking cage in a tarp
and loaded it in my car.

I drove. He stayed silent.
We drove through the next town across the river,
to the country club,
a little paradise, I thought.

I feared his teeth as I opened the trap
but he bolted, and galloped off in panicky loops,
a lost soul in a foreign land dotted with little dead-end holes

In my memory he's forever homeless,
waiting for me to come and return him to his burrow,
like a kid orphaned on the last day of summer camp.

But this is now. You are Omega's woodchuck,
and there is a measure of trust between us.
Soon we will sleep. I will think of you,
lulled by the familiar sounds and vibrations
of creatures tunneling the ground above and below,
click of beetle legs, rumble of mole plow.
Maybe you will hear under your quilt of loam,
a barely audible sound, the shifting crumbs of earth,
rootlets pressing down.

I Return as a Turtle from My Dreams

For weeks my dreams hid from me,
crouched, mum and sullen when I woke.

>*Still yourself*
>*Give your silent word*
>*Listen*

In the morning three words
inside a turtle shell:

>*Retrace   your   steps*

But I am literal, like a credulous kid
holding an empty conch to my ear.

Hearing no sea,
I go hunting for a turtle shell.
It arrives bubble-wrapped and boxed
from a man who claims he found it in the woods.
Unwrapped, it's a small leathery cabinet,
polished by time to a burnished glow.
Inside, carapace, plastron and scutes,
a little cave,
its floor swept clean by sow beetles and ants,
ceiling sprung by ribs of arched gray-white bone
like stalactites.
This was once a hatchling's body and home.
It grew with her flesh, moved with a heart that kept time.
Two lungs exhaled the musky breath of forest floor.

>*Listen*

A scratch and a shift,
four doors open, four sturdy oars deploy
and churn the chilly waters of spring and pond,
and then bearing her weight in slow steps,
laboring up to softer ground, to dig deep,
and entrust her cargo of round eggs
to the warmth of the sun.

Give your word

The shell rests lightly on the palm of my hand.
I enter the sacred cave.

Retrace your steps

This time, not in doubt or regret,
but with patience, and wonder.

They Tell You "Have a Good One"

leaving it open-ended.
Sometimes what the good is
depends on who shows up.

Yesterday,
one good frog, on a day
almost too cold for frogs,

and too rainy for us who go around on two feet.
I thought the frog was a dead leaf
lifted by a breeze,

until leaf
signaled life
with one good hop,

a small frog, the size of a date,
and camouflaged with filigree,
like white lichen on a black stone.

Your good
depends
on who you are.

If you be toad, salamander or frog
you need one good tunnel
to cross under the road

from vernal pond
to summer woods.

But whether you travel

on two feet or four,
where wars ravish the land,

you'd better have a tunnel,
a good one.
I hope you have a good one.

May you have many good ones.

For the Trees

I

A prayer

not just for the ancient ones revered with brass plaques,
like the *"Significant Tree"* down by the lake,
growing when the constitution was signed,

but for all the trees.

To you, unnamed silver maple, giant of my neighborhood,
companion to a hulking gambrel-roofed barn,
windows all but shot out by vandals, roof starting to cave,
the whole thing listing like a shipwreck—

Maple Tree, may you remain.

And including, all you ashes and Norway maples
developers put in some fifty years back,
shapely and graceful now.

Thanks be
for how you weave an emerald swath
of shade through the blocks,
softening the corners, the stacks of condo boxes.
You grew your handsome trunks
strong and muscular like thighs,
divided yourselves at the waist
to better bend arms to the wind.
Your leaves, a million mirrors that draw down the sun's gold,
turn silver before a storm.

You pass the voice of the seed-bearing wind
hand to hand as it rides the hills,
filling the lungs of every being that breathes.

May you strengthen your hold.

This is my prayer of thanks to you, my city's trees,
for your forbearance.
How you stand in your appointed places
keeping watch in your ranks,
single file, block by block.
You bless the litter, the parade of boots,
endure the flapping plastic bags snagged in your highest
    branches
like tattered flags of the nations,
your leaves deformed by devouring beetles,
sticky tents of hungry worms.
You welcome the nest-builders, the hole-dwellers,
bear your graffiti scars with dignity,
your wasted seed ground to dust under our feet.

In gratitude I rest my back against your roots.
I look up to you, kings and queens,
bless your offspring and your seed,
you, who give us life on this piece of stone,
hold us safe within our sun's loving pull,
this solitary place in a cold universe.

Forgive us for how we forget you
who do outlive us.

As much as is in my power,
in my small way, from this day forth
I vow I will protect you.

To the 9/11 "Survivor Tree"

Singular star of humble roots,
ordinary member of an invasive species, *Pyrus calleryana,*
Callery pear, propagated for blossoms that billow
like cumulous clouds in the spring, and pear-less-ness in the fall.
Landscapers and street sweepers love you.
Never once have you littered the sidewalks of New York with
    your fallen fruit.

In the moment before the firestorm,
your leaves were deep green and lush, your branches supple and
    smooth,
before the gale of ash and flame overtook you,
decapitated you,
cracked and blackened the bark of your trunk,
incinerated in an instant
your every twig and leaf.

But afterwards,
buried beneath the fallen canyons of caved concrete and
    contorted steel,
under the ground of Ground Zero,
your roots remained, alive and seeking.
For weeks, inside the conjoined columns of your xylem cells,
unbroken vessels,
you held the water of life,
until, unburied, you let its sweetness flow again
upwards toward the light, into your remaining stump.

It was October.
A tired worker paused

to notice you had put forth
a sprinkling of new leaves, dusty but green,
just as you had done every spring, that ordinary miracle.
He saw an injured being that might be loved back to health.
Nurserymen came to prune your roots, wrap you in burlap.
They didn't give up on you,
but carried you to a park in another borough,
fostered and tended you,
named you Survivor, as you slowly grew past your scars,
stretched out new branches,
became verdant and beautiful again.

And then they returned you
to this place of death and renewal.
We come here to grieve and remember,
celebrate life and love.
You show us how.
We thank you.

Forms of *Ahimsa*

I nearly kick it with my sneaker
but my brain's right side knows better—
not brown leaf but brown bat.
More curious than squeamish
I lean down to check its desiccated snout
for signs of fungus,
the disease that sickens the bats,
not us.

In the mountains of Haiti an elderly man told me
bats are old mice that grow wings,
like people become angels.
My friend Cata's neighbors just returned from California,
where they took pictures of angels.
They said they looked just like the ones in the old paintings.
"Which old paintings?" She's an art historian.
She wanted to know.
But they wouldn't show people their photos,
to protect the angels.
I thought it was supposed to be the other way around.
Maybe someone poisoned the bat
with warfarin, a mold that grows in damp hay,
and kills the cows,
a natural thing that became a commodity
and needed a name—
warfarin, or Coumadin,
a serviceable substance, for killing rats,
and saving humans with bad hearts.

It was another human, some four hundred years ago,
who examined a life and had a useful thought
about how things could go better.
It was just an observation,
but he assembled a euphonious little parcel of words, in Dutch,
something like we still say,
"Live and let live."
Some people still believe
if you let live
long enough
you grow wings.

Late September in the Anthropocene

At dawn, a pulsing
sound like a distant alarm

a single cricket,
just enough warmth in his wings
to muster his music.

I want to rise like that
with no thought of time

no word
of emergency.

I do not want to see
Earth as poisoned and maimed,

the body
as anything but perfect.

Study the way
Earth rights herself

one cricket, one song
given into a chilly dawn,

one seed
fallen to the ground,
from which nothing may emerge.

There is no trouble.
Others rise.

HAIKU

ᥫᩣ

THIRTEEN HAIKU

fallen tree blocks
my back gate
now only wild things come knocking

bean vines I train
to twine up my garden fence
never reach the sun

searching a vast store
for a new compass
finding only a compass

finches on zinnias
scattering half the seeds
more for next year

house finches' chatter
sibling squabbles
or cheers for the family flock

flock of starlings' whoosh
cicadas' crescendo
follows their decrescendo.

washing a window
glass pane between
two unmasked strangers

he paints tropical landscapes
in Vermont winter
I'm green with envy

donating blood in Covid
weighing risks
giving and receiving

sparrows in a box store
trick the electric eye
longing for sky

Ruth Bader Ginsburg
who can blame you for leaving
this fall—will we rise?

HAIBUN

❧

THREE HAIBUN

MEDICINE

Scott Peck was my dad's psychiatrist after a near-miss suicide attempt. Scott took him on as his only patient when he was writing his best seller, *The Road Less Traveled*. During that time my family came to think of "Scotty" as a sort of savior. It was an unorthodox mash-up of therapy, friendship, and witchcraft. He turned my cautious pediatrician dad onto pot. They attended an exorcism. For a while my dad's depression lifted. My one and only session with Scott was more conventional, a chat at his lakeside house in the Berkshires, where the late spring black flies were ferocious. As I swatted, he sat calm and unperturbed, as befitted his persona as a spiritual adept. Probably his bug-free state had more to do with the cloud of cigarette smoke which surrounded him. I smoked in my teens and twenties. I liked the little lift of nicotine, how it made me feel suave. I still miss cigarettes in mosquito season.

> after summer drought
> sweet sweet rain perfumes the air
> tobacco plants sigh

My flowering tobacco, *Nicotiana sylvestris*, is finally in bloom. Last summer's plants scattered their invisible seed all over the garden. In July the seedlings appear. I move some to the back, and share the rest with friends. In August, when the cucumber vines have mildewed, and the peony leaves are blotched with blight, the nicotianas are gorgeous goddesses, towering over the herbs and little patches of lettuce and chard. In the evening, their nodding clusters of white blossoms release a thick tropical scent to woo the pollinating moths.

> wide unmarred leaves
> shunned by flea beetle and slug
> not their medicine

TRUST

It's taken me months to dare leave the world's cutest dog in the food coop's "barking lot." This early Sunday morning the store is quiet, so I tie her to a plant rack near the door. Another old, masked, early-bird shopper looks on—

"Aren't you afraid someone will take your dog?"
"Well, I just can't live like that," I say.
She gets back in her car seething with righteous indignation. I decide to have faith in my neighbors and resume my shopping trip.

> gel hands, don gloves, wipe down cart
> take care, tongs, don't you bruise these
> tender shiitakes

When I come out, Dawn, my favorite bagger, is sitting next to my dog, rubbing her ears.

Back home, just as I switch off the lawn mower, a not-so-old woman appears on the sidewalk pushing a wheeled walker with a seat. She sits down on it to rest.

"Your lawn looks very pretty. Your flowers too. By the way, do you have a car?"

She needs a ride to the bank, which also happens to be my bank. It's turned out to be too long a walk for her. Blaming Covid, I decline.

She says she understands, "but I don't have the virus. We gotta trust each other."

I offer to run her bank errand, and she hands over her passport and a one hundred dollar check.

The teller, who has worked in the bank for years and is invariably calm and kind, makes allowances for the passport, expired by six years. He slides an envelope of cash under the plexiglass, along with the usual dog biscuit.

When I arrive at my new friend's group home, she is waiting for me on the porch, delighted to introduce me to her housemates.

"I know where you live now!" she calls as I drive away. "I'm going to bring you a reward!"

> chickadee perches
> and flies—big toe remembers
> clasp of wiry feet

QUAIL

In the Vietnamese grocery I buy a package of frozen quail. I
don't know why. I hardly ever buy meat. Maybe because they
remind me of a Frenchman I once knew who loved quail. I
remember I prepared them for him with herbs in their cavities
and bacon blankets.

When the package thaws the pink skinless bodies are nested,
severed necks to feathery feet in two rows of four. They're noth-
ing like birds. They are not little chickens. How could I have
forgotten how sad they look? How human. The first one lies
cool and limp in my hand, a headless homunculus. I insert the
rosemary sprig. It feels like rape, weird and necrophiliac. Then
the bacon shroud, flesh on flesh, red striped with white fat. I
have to finish this. I try to think I'm honoring the bodies with
old French culinary rituals. It would be much worse to throw
them in the garbage.

They cook in minutes in the sizzling hot oven—the recipe dic-
tates rare. The kitchen smells deep, rich, musky, and delicious,
drawing the dog to the oven door. But I can barely manage to
eat even one. It's impossible to use a knife and fork. I have to
pull the meat off the bone with my teeth. I remember I'm a
predator, and feel something like shame. I make a plan to con-
ceal the evidence. Tomorrow make soup. Nice yellow potatoes,
mushrooms, butternut squash.

> iron pot steeps
> fire purifies
> bone strengthens bone

Tea Boy

Before he left India to bring Buddhism to Tibet
Atisha selected his monks.

His choice of the tea boy,
notorious for his obnoxious and abrasive ways,
caused the others to ask, *why?*

But Atisha had heard the rumor—
Tibetans were gracious and good-hearted all.
He feared he'd get lazy,
lose his spiritual muscle
without the tea boy
to press his buttons.

My tea boy has followed me here,
to a silent retreat in the desert outside Oracle, Arizona.

She plays her part with rigor and consistency
from her mat next to mine in the zendo.

She lies down to meditate
and promptly erupts in snores.
She comes in late in the morning, wearing pink pajamas,
sits on her cushion and applies her lipstick.

Each day she perfects new ways to peeve me.

She slurps her coffee
and sloshes it on the floor.
All day I can count on her
to break the Noble Silence and ask ignoble questions—

"Tell me, that white-haired gentleman who fixed the toilet,
is he your husband?"

On the last day of retreat
I secretly pay for her massage,
though I fear it could work too many miracles,
and I'm not done here yet.

I leave the desert
and arrive three hours early
for a stay in Madera Canyon.
Relaxed and happy
I putter about the cabin unpacking,
arranging my little bags of food in the cupboards,
my shoes neatly by the door.

A woman named Sue comes in
with a bucket and broom.

I see on her tired face
my presence has interrupted the peace of her work,
and all my friendliness and apologies
annoy her, like an over-friendly puppy.

I see
her tea boy
has arrived right on time.

After Vodou at the Fleming Museum

I rummage in my closet,
find an old white dress, a half-full bottle of rum,
stick five bucks in my pocket to get in the door.
But we are welcomed as we are,
ill-at-ease, up-for-it, or somewhere in between,
invited to dance with two mambos and the drums.

> Papa Legba, here is rum I brought you.
> It's five-star Barbancourt. Won't you take a taste?
> Lord of the crossroads, if I could pray,
> would you hear my words?
> Can you read my thoughts in translation?

On this my first date with the lwa,
I cannot be the virgin bride, my lamp filled with oil,
but I move my hips and feet in step with Mambo Maude.
I want the dance to teach me something
maybe too late to learn—
too little time—no one's fault
the museum has to close by eight.

> Erzulie Dantor, do you remember me?
> Are you at home at this resplendent table?
> Do your feet feel cold on the marble floor?
> And all these luminous things, fit for princes and queens,
> made of peacock feathers, sequins and beads,
> starting to pulse—
> can you feel their heat?

To me they whisper
touch us
please

DO NOT TOUCH

speak the labels taped to the walls

My hand would never touch these consecrated things,
but they touch me.
Ever since, all I see
are altars.

Altars on dashboards,
altars in stores,
altars by the counter at the take-out Thai,
altars at roadsides,
for the missing and slain,
rumors of altars made by mole-folk underground
where lost keys and coins fall
through subway grates,
and are sanctified.

And in a place that is my home for now,
dismantled altars wait for me,
displaced in basement boxes and bureau drawer.
They wait for me this day,
as I set my Thanksgiving table.
Bouquet of barberry, roses and pine,
my hand mirrored in a silver bowl
lit by gold beeswax spires.

Flame touches wick,
everything shimmers
in this altered light.

Palomas in San Miguel

In the wild garden outside my door
rocks have faces.
Little black birds skim over the treetops
flashing vermillion,
and the tyrant kiskadee shrieks,
pilfering eggs from unguarded nests.

But it's the doves who dwell here,
cooing their monotonous tune at the first hint of dawn,
old couples who never leave home,
murmuring their prayers,
give us this day …

Some nights the troubled dogs don't sleep.
They pass their Doppler shift of warning along the walls.

I plug my ears and clamp the windows tight,
leave them closed in the morning.
It's cold, and the gas heater is useless.
Only the touch of the drunken landlady's finger will ignite it.

I make coffee in the one pot I have
and refill it to wash my nightgown,
stand on a chair in the garden
to hang it from a tree branch.

Morning warms the stones on the street.
Old men and gringos hobble by
watching their feet on the cobbles.
Dogs sleep in the sun as I pass by
on my way down the hill.

In the square the Parroquia's facade is lit
pink and frothy as sugar on a wedding cake.
Cypress trees and organ cactus
steeple up to a sky of delphinium blue.
In the market I fill my bag.
Handfuls of tiny tomatoes and red speckled beans,
one huge onion, white as a moon.

In the evening I make soup,
refill the pot to wash my bowl and cup,
and remember my nightgown still hanging in the tree.
I teeter on a chair
and reach up into the dark—
the touch of my hand
sparks an explosion of doves.
Wings whistle and flap
like gloved hands clapping.
The doves flee into the night,
and there is no way to call them back.
I can only bless them from my bed,
wrapped in my nightgown
that smells of leaves and rain.

I sleep and dream of my children.
In my dream family
they are also children of others,
at play on the backs of a cold sea
where blackbirds huddle,
dragging limp wings spattered with salt.

At dawn I hear the doves.
They've come home.

Paloma, paloma,
they sing. We are here.
We were never far away.

In Marseille

I am one of the many unaccounted victims
of the Imp of the Perverse.
Edgar Allan Poe

Standing by an unscreened window four stories up,
floor-to-ceiling opening a Goliath could stride through,
there's nothing to stop you.

It isn't that you want to fling yourself out
or the baby you adore like the moon,
but your body thins and feels light in a way
that could be risky under certain circumstances—
distraction, touch of mania, alcohol or indica.

You're drawn to stand at the lip of this wide, blue sea
where pigeons fly in aimless arcs
away over the sleeping Ferris wheel
and the ship masts in the old port.

Marseille woke up hours ago
and now is dozing back to sleep in the midmorning sun.
You want a closer look—too close!
The sting of the imp zings and tingles
from heart to fingertips,
needles down to the soles of your feet.

You could fly! You must step away
or your arms might let go and pour out
like a pitcher of milk onto the stone square below.
Of course, you will not do the unspeakable thing.
You hold the baby closer,
and perch your hip on the corner of the breakfast table

next to the spoons and coffee cups,
and the plate of flat bread and fig jam,
your legs safely weighted by your wiser bones.

And there must be some unknowable code
that keeps the pigeons from flying in the windows,
unaware that they are angels, and would be welcome at your table.
They fly in circles over the square below,
and settle on the roof of the old hotel.
They stand around and wait, and sail again,
you believe, all through the day,
after you've gone off and forgotten them.

At dusk, on the Quai des Belges
there are dancers and drums, and a tall dark-haired man
standing off to one side, dressed like a Rom,
with a falcon perched on his shoulder.
The bird's eyes and the man's survey the crowd.
There must be a tether that holds the falcon there,
but you don't see it.

Snow-Brush

Snow sifts through or settles on branches.
The world cleansing itself,
its infinite distinctions erased,
the common air becoming to your eyes
visible, crystalline, pooling
into wells of blue,
the world finally sensible,
recognizable. You remember you
have always known this
is how it would look.

And this is how you create your world at dawn:
lighting a candle, a stick of forty-minute incense,
standing it up in a bowl of sand.
Still, as the body settles, the mind
mines the world for some spark of novelty,
flies off with the least little sparrow
on the other side of the window,
tries to forget the taste of last night's over-salty soup.

It isn't necessary to erase a thing. Letting go,
thoughts pass with the gentleness of a feather duster.
Enough to emulate the precision of a raindrop
piercing the surface of a pond.
Memories, plots and plans, all things could dissolve.

You recall yesterday's drive home,
King Street in the late afternoon,
passing a car shrouded in snow.
Some ghost of a finger has jabbed dark letters

across the windshield.
The word   FAG   aims its menace
at passing cars and pedestrians.

This time, you know what to do.
With one snow-brush stroke
hate dies so easily,
the snow is so light.

At the ICE Building

188 Harvest Lane, Williston, Vermont

1

We sit here Wednesdays at 5,
along a strip of roadside grass
in a line, like people waiting for a parade.
Not long ago there were fields here,
corn for the harvest,
barns full of Holsteins.
Now it's a Monopoly board of box stores and banks,
cradle to grave, Toys R Us.
And this place we didn't know,
never noticed, until we knew,
harbors the operations of ICE.

We sit on the ground,
chill starting to seep into our legs,

eyes open, eyes closed,
some with cardboard signs propped against their knees.

I am an empty-handed witness with no words.

Nothing to see here.
Security guard strolling the lot,
two-thirds empty at evening shift.
Monolithic building, built of gray bricks,
anonymous by design,
locked-down and defended
by concrete blocks like a row of teeth.

I can tell you the windows lie.
They mirror back a sky of charcoal and blue,
trees turning gold in the slant fall light.

I sit with only questions drifting by,
no one to ask.
The children, where are they now?
Does anybody know
how their empty-handed mothers sleep?

2

Sometimes someone driving by honks
a few staccato beeps, sounding like thanks
in the language of cars.

Last week a woman, old like me, pulled out of the lot,
the gate's arm lifting and sinking to release her.
She rolled down her window to speak.
"You have to trust God," she said,
and pointed to the badge hanging from her neck,
as if the face of God were on it.

 She said it twice again as she drove away—
You have to trust God, trust God,
as if this had been her mantra all through the day
while she did what she does with the data.
Did her god listen in when someone called the tip line
to report the presence of three brown-skinned men
in a Northeast Kingdom Walmart,
where they went to wire their wages home?

When the men were detained,

who milked the cows?
Did the money make it home?
Do the kids have milk?

3

It gets dark now as we sit
bundled in blankets, lanterns lit beside our signs
a few cars slow down to read.
A big man leaving the building in a white pickup
has to wait for traffic, aiming his headlights at our eyes.
And then he dims them,
a kindness in the language of cars,
or at least it says, *I see you.*

When he goes home to watch TV, eat his dinner and sleep,
have the *migrantes* begun their long march?
Will their children sleep tonight?
The gods they pray to,
do they forgive us?

Bird and Wall

Catbird rockets into woods' edge,
piercing the milk-green wall at full tilt,
the way flocks of sparrows sieve themselves en masse
through chain-link fences,
like a spray of water.

I complain to a friend, I want to write about that,
but the tropes get in the way—
biblical sparrows flying free over ancient walls.
I want to see each bird in the instant it folds its wings
to fit inside the little tilted square of wire
and stretches wide again as its tail slips free.

But here, a nine-year-old boy listening in, says,
That's not hard, I could write about that.
And it isn't hard for him
to sift through all the words he knows.
His poem will enter with a whoosh
and vanish without a trace or an epitaph,
some version of Kilroy was here,
poking his cartoon nose over the wall.

Birds leave nothing,
no lingering touch, no stray feathers snag
as they pass over razors and barbs.
Even if I resist the symbol-making urge—
paloma and eagle carving circles over newly built walls,
the eyes of border cams scanning the valleys and hills,
fresh paint sprayed over dry blood—

words have already begun their work of hemming in,
and must adjust to fit the next moment's truth.

Feathers will be lost,
animals of all kinds harmed.

What I want to know is,
when the lion lies down with the lamb,
what is between them?

FIVE PROSE PIECES

❧

I

WE ASK THE DOCENT AT THE KENT'S CORNER MUSEUM FOR OTHER PLACES TO VISIT AND HE GIVES US DIRECTIONS TO A SMALL ASHRAM WHOSE NAME HE CAN'T REMEMBER

First you get yourselves to Curtis Pond. So you go down past the old mill and turn right at the Maple Corners store, and then turn right again, and left, so you're on the Worcester Road, I don't know if it's marked—it could be the West County road for a little ways—when you get to the pond you're gonna leave it on your right, past the swim beach and the boat access, and then you'll go uphill for a while and then come down—curving to the right and left maybe three times—it's a gravel road, like a tunnel, nice birches arching over, gold leaves falling—go slow, there's no sign or anything, just look for an old apple orchard, just five or six trees, but they keep it all mowed around, and that's where the path starts. Park on the other side, there's a little wooden bridge over a stream, more like a ditch—and up in the woods on that side is where they have their houses and gardens—a few people still live up there—but start at the orchard. Take the path into the woods. Go across a small stone bridge, with a sign that asks you to be quiet. They keep the woods picked up like a little park, with carpets of moss and periwinkle. They have a temple, you'll see it—bit run down, but someone's been working on it. And there's a meditation cave—you can go inside. It has a chimney, but covered up with leaves and things growing out of the roof, so you wouldn't know there's a cave with a fire burning inside unless you smell the smoke—but you'll see the door. The light switch is on your

right, or you can follow the glow from the hearth. There's cushions on the
rocks, a couple chairs—you can sit as long as you like.

Well. That's how we got there. But no one can prepare you for
the silence.

II

QUESTIONS ABOUT THE FUTURE USE OF THE NAME ENGLESBY BROOK IN THE ABSENCE OF THE BROOK ITSELF

Brook: a body of running water flowing in a natural channel.
Watershed: an area of land drained by a river or other body of water.

Body: the physical structure of a person or animal,

If a human body lacks certain parts, such as a hand, gall
bladder, or kidney, it is still a human body. But if it lacks a head
or heart, is it human? Is it an immortal body?
If a brook, which by definition flows through a natural channel,
no longer has a channel, is it still a brook?

If Englesby Brook no longer flows through its natural channel, is
it Englesby Brook?

If a river is diverted and made to run through an engineered
channel, it is said to be not a river, but a canal. If Englesby
Brook flows through metal pipes and concrete conduits, what is
it? If Englesby Brook's water no longer flows, but is contained in
an excavated hole, what is this body?

If Englesby Brook's channel ran through a ravine in a woodland which no longer exists since the trees were cut and the land leveled, what is this place?

If the water passing through the region formally known as the Englesby Brook watershed no longer drains into a brook but an engineered water system, what is this land?

What is the word for a nameless body?

Nameless: anonymous, unremembered, unrecognized, forgotten

III

ON THE RED-EYE READING
LILLIAN BOXFISH TAKES A WALK

I turn the last page, and close it with a sigh. If I have really loved a book, I set it on my coffee table for a while, and feel its sparkle as I pass by. After Kathleen Rooney's *Lillian Boxfish Takes a Walk*, it was many months before I could pack it up and send it off to my sister Barbara. She is recovering from a health crisis and needs a good book. I don't expect her to return it. She may not love it, or even read it. My sister Eloise had lent me the book this summer, before she drove me to PDX to catch the last New York flight. She said she'd liked it, sounding a bit tepid. I wondered if she'd finished it—a telltale bookmark somewhere near the middle. I didn't sleep a wink, reading all night. Six months later, I still think about Lillian Boxfish. It sounds crazy, but I felt that she needed me to read her story.

When I meet her, I'm in the middle seat between a sleepy

marine and a guy in a hoodie and earbuds. Lillian has just stepped out of her Manhattan apartment building at 22 East 36th street, in the Murray Hill neighborhood, about an hour's walk from where my sisters and I grew up. Boxfish, elegant in a mink coat and blue fedora, wishes the doorman a happy New Year. It's the late afternoon of her 86th New Year's Eve. Not long into her walk she ducks into a nearly empty neighborhood bar for a Negroni. I feel a twinge of worry about her drinking alone and on an empty stomach, except for the half bag of Oreos she doesn't remember buying. But she has already begun to charm me with her tales of New York in the 1930s, and I'm hooked.

Kathleen Rooney's note in the back of the book tells me she based her novel on the actual life of Margaret Fishback, a feminist before there was a word for it, who had a lucrative and successful career in the nearly all-male advertising world of her day. What's more, she wrote and published light verse, which was all the rage at a time when mainstream readers actually bought and read books of poetry. Rooney's Lillian charms me, like a delightful new friend, way out of my IQ league, with a cutting wit, something like Dorothy Parker, but capable of generosity and kindness to strangers. On her New Year's Eve walkabout, Lillian's style and honesty disarm the motley collection of people she encounters, including a family dining at Delmonico's. They invite Lillian to join them after the hostess has turned her away for lack of a reservation. But when she disappears after a trip to the powder room I start to worry again. I follow her out the door and into the mostly deserted financial district. I'm wide awake and tensely upright in my cramped seat, witnessing her run-in with three young would-be muggers somewhere near the Port Authority. After some negotiation with one of them, she persuades him to hand over his track jacket in trade for her mink coat. The night is cold. I shiver with her in the thin jacket. She has lost her beloved coat. I have lost all track of time.

I'm nearly two-thirds into the 284-page book before the wall around Lillian the witty raconteur begins to crack. Wait—have I missed some trail of breadcrumbs hinting at a looming break-down? In the middle of a Sunday night, seven miles above the American Midwest, a large chunk of her life begins to fall off. I'm bracing for the crash.

But what moves me and leaves me blowing my nose as best I can without disturbing my seatmates, is the feeling that I'm learning the unvarnished truth of her life because I have earned her trust. This is so strange. How does one earn the trust of a fictional character? Suddenly, devastatingly, with 22 pages left to go, my new friend allows me to witness her terrible act of self-destruction.

I think, how odd is this? Almost anyone with five bucks, a phone and an Amazon account can buy a used copy of *Lillian Boxfish Takes a Walk*, in acceptable condition. But six months after reading the book, I still treasure this strange feeling of privilege. Because I walked all night with her, and stayed with her when she was broken and lost, she chose to entrust me with the true story of her life.

IV

MY NEIGHBOR OMAR

When he was young he was a dancer. He studied at the Hostos Center for the Arts in the Bronx. He's still young, way too young for two bad hips and a stroke—too young to spend his days in a wheelchair, parked in front of the co-ops. When he came to Vermont, he told me, he worked in the OR as an instrument specialist."I was good at it," he said, "but they had to let me go." *Let* him go? As if he wanted to go. What he does now is worry. Sometimes there isn't enough food for him and his wife. You have to be over sixty-five to get Meals On Wheels. The neighborhood helps. People bring him sandwiches from City Market. He likes the breakfast sandwiches from the hot bar, and the custom-made ones from the deli, with a bottle of juice.

"I'm not begging," he says, tears spilling from his brown eyes. Then he flips into laughter at the sight of my dog instigating a spat with two cats in the window of the basement apartment next door.

"The lady across the street doesn't like me," he says. She told him, "I don't always feel like saying hi." She thinks he's looking in her kitchen window.

"Hey," I say, "that's what curtains are for. Anyway, Omar, it's her loss." Because, truth is, the rest of the neighborhood depends on him for free hugs. Rain or shine.

Yesterday he was out in a miserably cold drizzle. Most of us could use a hug on these dark December days. This morning it's sunny, and with his sleeves rolled up he looks strong. But he's worrying about money again, and the long winter coming on. One time the People's Kitchen brought him food, but they never came back. His food stamp application keeps getting mailed to the wrong address. I try to help. CVOEO doesn't return my calls either. He's still waiting for a social worker to replace the one who left during covid. I can only imagine his loneliness during that long covid winter.

Last week, in my basement one block away, I was cleaning up, putting stuff out on the street with a "free" sign. I happened to look out my front door at the moment a delighted couple discovered my old cast iron pot, the one I can no longer lift with one hand. I sold my old backcountry skis on Front Porch Forum for 100 bucks. The cash sat on my desk for a few days until I stuck it in a holiday card and addressed it to Omar. He was visiting with a ponytailed young man when I walked by, carrying the envelope in my pocket, so I slipped it into the pouch on the back of his chair. This morning when I drive by I see Omar is out, despite the dark clouds and biting wind. He spots me, and waves, flashing a grin that lights up the gloom.

V

TO A BUDDHIST NUN ON THE PLUM VILLAGE
YOUTUBE CHANNEL

Thank you for your invitation to come home to the island within myself. I hope to get to my island soon. But first I would like to ask you a favor. Could I just stop by for a brief visit to yours? I can imagine it, the very quiet island of your mind, inside your freshly shaven, beautifully sculpted head. Actually I'm headed out to your island right now—you can probably see me, with my pants rolled up, wading out through the turquoise water, with a school of little fish sparkling around my feet. I promise I won't stay long. I would just like to sit and watch the butterflies and bees in your lovingly tended garden. Maybe we'll have some tea, followed by a short nap under your solitary yew tree, with its graceful bonsai shape. After a nap, I believe I will be ready to venture out to my island. It's rocky out there. My island is buffeted by wind and rising tides. On sunny days, it's plagued by sportfishing boats and tourists on jet skis. I prefer it on rainy days, when I have it to myself. The sound of the rain almost drowns out the roar of the fighter bombers hidden in the clouds. After they pass, I sit for a few moments, enjoying the rain falling on the island inside myself.

Maps and Games

for Sue Burton

Every day we make a new map.
The old ones don't match the coordinates
on an infected globe.
Big Mama's thrown us a spit ball,
our orbit's off-kilter. Catch it if you can.
We're playing the game we call statues,
barefoot on a summer lawn.
My big sister's always It,
spinning us around one by one by an arm,
and cutting us loose, whirling away
and landing in frozen poses.
She picks the one who looks the most like Yogi Berra,
but really she always chooses her best friend.
And then we play a wild and reckless kick-the-can,
huddling in the dark woods and running like crazy back to home
    base.

Last night, as the dark settled over the quiet neighborhood,
I heard a kid call out a few blocks away,
Ollie, Ollie, in come free!
In the game of tag you make a human chain
linked to home base,
bringing your friends to safety,
some kind of electric current passed
hand to hand.

Who knows? Tomorrow
maybe row row row your boat
between the pirañas, hot lava, and sharks.

We'll sing to them sweetly,

Ollie
Ollie
in come free

We'll row and row
to an island we call home.
If you don't touch anyone
it's called safety.

Acorn

Acorn: Related to the Old English aecern (modern acre). Ultimately acorn evolved to mean something akin to "fruit of the unenclosed land."

Lumpy cargo bulging a winter-ready squirrel's cheeks,
and a combat-ready kid's sweatshirt pouch.
Draw a face on your finger, add an acorn cap,
and a comrade appears in a patterned hat,
to help you kindle your tale.
Construct a tiny house out of bark,
with an oak-leaf bed and a mossy quilt.
Put an ear to the ground.
Acorns have been known to talk in their sleep.

The past five nights our neighborhood trees are rich with new
    fruit,
the dark bodies of a thousand roosting crows,
restless and noisy like a stadium crowd.
I go out and ask them why they chose our trees.
I get no answers.
But today I rise before dawn to watch them leave,
a rising cacophony of caws before a group of them lifts,
and as they fly off, they lightly touch their outstretched wings,
tip to tip, like football players fist-bumping.

We call our backyard trees invasive,
like us, the trees that sprout on disturbed land,
black locust, Norway maple, buckthorn, half-choked by
    bittersweet vine.
Once this was a valley of tall, tall trees,
vast forests of giant oaks, maples, hickory and pine.

When travelers on horseback passed under,
the lowest branches were far above their reach,
in the time before the treaties were made and broken,
before the felling of the unmeasured trees,
when flocks of a billion carrier pigeons darkened the sky.

Will we evolve a word to mean
the unenclosed land we have to find inside ourselves?

I ask the crows.
I don't expect an answer,
but I carry the question like an acorn in my pocket.

On the Bus

After Elizabeth Bishop's "In the Waiting Room"

In nineteen fifties New York City
a third grader could ride the crosstown bus alone,
having learned to evade the unzipped men in the park,
and the candy store owner on eighty-fourth street
barking obscenities into a backroom telephone.
I knew I should leave, but I wanted my Mounds bar.
His words burrowed through my eardrums like maggots,
as if I deserved them.

But on a late-winter afternoon,
nothing was happening on a crosstown bus that smelled of wet
    wool
and a bag of five-and-dime-store popcorn spilled at my feet.
A little man with a trim mustache
dozed over his neatly folded *El Mundo*,
until he reached his stop and rose
sleepwalking to the back door that wheezed open for him.
New riders ascended at the front,
women in pairs clinked their quarters and dimes
and moved to the rear as told to,
sighing into seats or stood leaning ear into elbow,
like sloths hanging from the overhead bar.

Halfway back, from the little island of my seat
a new thought startled my mind—
I looked out at all the heads
inside their knitted caps and felt homburgs,
and was given to know that inside each one

there were thoughts and words
passing through, just as my own flowed by
on their way to somewhere or to dissolve into something else.
It was like finding a key to a secret room
on the other side of a door I hadn't noticed before.

I can't say if this knowledge elevated or changed me.
To this day I'm still at the mercy
of whom or what it is that keeps the keys.

Hail Marys, a Villanelle

While mating close to the time of egg laying leads to more success, some males find the benefits of breeding at the sanctuaries to outweigh the costs. These males are typically in the poorest condition. They often have diminished wing state and small abdomens (which means less fat reserve). They are least likely to survive the migration to Texas. Males in better condition and more capable of surviving the migration will likely choose differently. For male monarchs, breeding in Mexico is sort of a Hail Mary.

~From Bicycling with Butterflie*s by Sara Dykman*

It's all Hail Marys from here on out
though it's monarchs not men
she's talking about.

Survivors of sleet storms, gales and draught,
he'll catch her and mate her he will, if he can.
But it's all Hail Marys from here on out,

because for monarchs and humans, time's running out.
Their wings are all holey, our cheeks, all wan.
It's the last grasp we're talking about.

Of this, one's offspring would rather not talk about.
They cringe at the plans
of these geriatric gadabouts

with nothing to lose, nor regrets to fret about,
spending their savings on vacations in Cannes,
or was it Spain? What's this about?

Not a whimper, it's a shout!
Not quite what they'd want, but all they can
muster. It's all Hail Marys from here on out.
Float or flounder, a winged thing this love is about.

Boys

In my all-girl world,
three blocks, between home and school,
including the park and the "boardwalk" by the river,
you were free to walk alone,
or with your sisters and your girlfriends.
Even the Siamese cats, who never left home,
and lived out their days seven floors up,
were girls.

Out back in the courtyard
we played jump rope, with Band-Aids on our knees,
baseball with Rawlings mitts, and a pink rubber ball.
I couldn't hit
but miraculously, could pitch.
Our captain was a girl named PJ,
who much later switched
and became a boy named Pete.
There were boys in the courtyard, whose names I don't
    remember.

In my all-girl world, boys weren't quite third wheels,
more like training wheels,
always throwing things off balance,
tipping first to one side and then to the other—
one minute red-faced and yelling,
then silent when you asked them why.
Boys seemed like puppies tossed up in the air,
legs flailing until they landed and ran off somewhere.

My school was presided over by women in tweed suits
who ruled by their brilliance.
Twice a day, under the stern gaze of Miss Carling and Miss King,
we ran and leapt and kicked,
climbed ropes up to the ceiling,
and wondered about the funny feeling
it gave us between our legs.

We never thought of being better
than the mostly absent boys.
And when the newly pubescent Farrell boys
one floor down,
who rarely left their apartment and their three TVs,
invited my sister and me
to watch them jerk off in the basement,
they seemed like deranged zoo chimps
with nothing else to do.

The school up the street, PS 151,
dark brick, and dirty,
had two signs over its entrance doors,
BOYS & GIRLS
I imagined there were tunnels
leading to their pink and blue homerooms.

It wasn't until I met my friend Kitty's brother, Dickie
(in those days kids had names like Kitty and Dickie),
I discovered a curious kind of boy.
And their dad, Dr. Duane,
I loved for being unlike my own
(Daddy fumed behind the wheel of his Ford Fairlane
cursing traffic on the Major Deegan).

Kitty's dad would say to the car ahead, lollygagging in the left
    lane,
"Move over, friend," like the dad in *Father Knows Best*.

Dickie had a menagerie in his bedroom,
so many little mice and furry hamsters on exercise wheels,
it made you dizzy when you went in there at night.
And two giant speckled rabbits, who hopped around your legs
and the legs of the dining table during family meals.
In my mind Dickie was Dickon,
the Yorkshire lad in *The Secret Garden*,
who knew what part of a rose vine was *wick*,
meaning good and greenly alive.
Dickie would climb up to the highest branch of the tree
to peer into the bird nest for you,
and while he was up there, hang from his knees.
I loved everything he did.

But a few years later
I learned the meaning of cool
when Bob, my sister's tall boyfriend,
who exuded a mysterious, supernatural boy-grace,
leapt into the driver's seat of his convertible bug
without opening the door.

After that things got complicated.
Maybe it was because their carelessly beguiling banter
made my mother laugh like a girl,
she let us drive away with those boys.
I'll never know why she let us go.
We never came back.

Pollywogs

The swim class lines up at the deep end,
elbows to ears, all goggle-eyed and knob-kneed,
toes curled over the lip, awaiting a whistle
and a word from a woman
with a dolphin tattoo that ripples
with the band of muscles across her back.
The kids are six coiled springs, cocked and poised,

READY   SET   GO

The whistle's shriek ricochets off the concrete walls,
six small bodies are smacked and swallowed
by the element they suddenly remember to be their first home,
recall how it shaped them, weightless in spiraling movements,
how it felt to swim in pure love.
They dive down, propelled by their wriggling tails,
they seem to have no bones as they slither into shadows.

Their mothers' eyes search for them,
but their mucilaginous bodies have grown transparent,
reeds and silt conspire to hide them.
The mothers, who gave them lungs they no longer need,
stand landlocked and powerless like peacocks,
holding out flowery towels the children no longer need or see.
Until one spots her boy as he skims by just below the surface,
and she gathers all her mammalian love and fury, half-pleading,
half-growling down at him in a desperate and terrible voice

N   O   W

I   AM   TELLING   YOU

GET OUT OF THAT POOL

RIGHT NOW

ONE   TWO   THREE

and I only want the boy to dive back down
before it's too late,
before the net is cast,
and he is landed.

Visitor

for Finn

You arrive
just before your first birthday.
You eschew the bright colored plastic toys
set out in a basket
on the living room floor
next to the pile of musty smelling picture books
your mama once loved.
What you love is the soup pot on the back deck
filled to the brim with water from the hose,
a ladle and a cup.
You leave behind
small wet footprints.
They last a few seconds
in the bright morning sun.
Later, we go to the mountains
to the cabin built by the great uncles
and their drinking buddies.
They called it
The Crow Hole.
We call it The Shack,
or, fondly,
Bug Bite.
You explore an old mouse nest,
peruse the woodpile,
practicing your pincer grasp
on the big black carpenter ants.
You wear a half-squashed ant for a while
on the front of your tee shirt.

The morning of our departure
it's your birthday.
Your papa goes out to dig a hole,
searching between the rocks and tree roots
for a place the shovel will go down.
Finally, in the middle of the path to the lake,
he digs a fine round hole.
Your mama unwraps a plastic box
which once held Brooklyn Chinese take-out
and now holds your placenta,
which has been in the freezer for a year
and thawed in the backpack
your papa carried here on the train.
This thing of flesh and connection
now re-emerges,
portentous, ripe,
in a pool of dark blood we do not touch.
It was once a stream of three strands,
the place on earth where you began
to deposit your alluvium,
began your forever
fanning out.

This outlived thing
we need to bury now
or its roots will die.
We bury it in hope
it will hold you here.
Your papa replaces the mound of loam.
We scatter leaves and pine needles
as if we were trying to hide the evidence
of our prying into secrets below.

And you, the birthday child,
begin to travel
up and down the path.
Your bare feet
press lightly,
leaving no marks on the old ground.

Home Birth

for Django

It was hot in Brooklyn
the summer you were born
in an old brick building,
five flights up.
The evening you were born
your mama paced
the long hallway
between the bedroom and kitchen,
bare feet padding the wooden floor,
sounding its reliable creaks.
Your brother, Finn,
four days shy of three years old,
and I, your grandmother,
wandered down Eastern Parkway
to Franklin Street,
past the little man sitting on his stoop,
talking with an island lilt
to us and to his canaries and finches
in cages hanging from a no-parking sign.
We were walking to the Botanic Garden,
seeking the coolness of the oak grove.
The summer you were born
it was an August
when the seventeen-year cicadas emerged,
crawling up from the ground,
leaving their dry husks everywhere,
and unfurling green-veined
clear glass wings.

Everywhere in the shadows,
their choruses crescendoed
like the shaking of ancient castanets.
Your brother heard this sound
as he fell asleep on a bench
beneath the great oaks.
And above our heads, above the trees,
three blocks away,
your mama still walked
down the hall,
and back again ...
The midwife followed,
wrapping her arms around
to hold up the heavy belly.
Your papa brought bowls of ice,
lit candles by the bed,
where you would soon be born.
Your sleeping brother and I returned,
and he lay a few hours
in a neighbor child's bed.
And another neighbor,
one flight down,
the one who used to pound his broom
and complain about the noise of little feet
running on the floor above his head,
the one who went away for a while to his motherland
on the island of Hispaniola.
There, he was shaken by earthquake and hunger,
and returned to Brooklyn
a changed and quieter man.
The night you were born,

he brought *lambi* and fried plantains,
red beans and rice,
in glass bowls covered with neatly ironed
white cloths.
Later in the evening,
you finally slipped free,
swimming up into the warm night air,
a perfect boy baby,
you opened your eyes
and took your first swallow of milk on this earth.
Your brother woke up and came upstairs,
and we all sat on the bed
eating the spicy food,
lifting glasses of cold champagne
to welcome you.
We looked into your wide dark eyes
that seemed to already know us.
Later,
in the quiet of the early morning,
you and your brother asleep in the big bed
between your parents,
I lay on the narrow cot in your papa's office,
and closed my eyes.
I could hear wind in the trees
and from the street below
the voices of people going by.
I imagined seventeen years from now,
two handsome young men,
brothers, walking home,
new rhythms in your footsteps.
Above your heads,

the cicadas have returned,
and are singing
in the tall tall trees.

Pickle's Bee

With the uncorrupted logic and faith of a six-year-old
the boy tends to the injured bee.
Any single thing at a time can be fixed.

His name is Zephyr, but everybody calls him Pickle.
When he was four, his love of birds prevented him from eating
    them.
No chicken fingers with his fries, no Thanksgiving drumsticks.
He tells me, *now there's a problem with the bees.*

It's possible he doesn't know
we're the cause of their dwindling.
In this case, a likely collision with a windshield or tire,
the trucked-in tractor mower that roared around the yard this
    morning.

The family doesn't own a lawn mower.
They're members of the latest migration,
driven by covid, climate, and nature hunger.
Until last week solid Brooklynites,
four little-to-bigger boys spooked by things that creep, crawl, and
    bite,
though we'd tried our best, giving them microscopes, ant farms,
    and sea monkeys,
lugged the pet tortoise to graze in Prospect Park.

The bee can't fly. She creeps and topples on a flagstone,
dragging a wing and hind leg with its pollen basket heavy with
    saffron dust.

He brings her a white clover blossom, and she instantly dives in
    like any bee
unfurling her wiry tongue, dipping into each little tube of
    sweetness.
She relishes a chive blossom too.

I tell him the wise flowers have chosen their colors just to please
    the eyes of bees.
He surrounds her with pink and white blooms, like a fairy ring,
where she stays all through the day and into a night of dancing
    fireflies,
barred owls calling back and forth from the woods.

In the chilly dawn I go out to check on the bee.
She's sluggish but still alive in her ring.
I resist the urge to make her disappear, as if she'd recovered and
    flown.

When the boy gets up we bring her fresh flowers.
But in the afternoon, a strong south wind blows in
and sweeps away the flowers and the bee.
That's good, Zephyr called Pickle says.
That's how she flies.

Acknowledgments

I feel tremendous gratitude for my writing friends who have given me valuable feedback on my poems, especially Emily Stribling, Sue Burton, Laurie Crosby, JoAnna Easton, and always Marylen Grigas, whose sweet supportive voice is still in my ear.

More gratitude for Michael Breiner and the posse at Flynndog, for providing a welcoming space for reading in Burlington, Vermont, and the poetry circle at Casa de la Noche in San Miguel de Allende.

My great appreciation to Judyth Hill and Mary Meade at Wild Rising Press. Without their kind help and great expertise, *Post & Line* would still be a bunch of poems gathering virtual dust inside my laptop.

Anne Damrosch's poems have appeared in *Solamente en San Miguel*, *The Baltimore Review*, *Nimrod International Journal*, *New Millennium Writings*, *Inquiring Mind*, *Heartfire: Second Revolutionary Poets Brigade Anthology*, among others. Her chapbook, *Entering the Story*, was published in 2012 by Finishing Line Press, Georgetown, Kentucky.

Finally, I would like to thank Kristin Urie for letting me use her wonderful painting for the cover of *Post & Line*. The day I drove to her farm on a back road in Vermont's Northeast Kingdom, hurricane Beryl was producing torrential rain and rising flood-waters. It was 100 percent worth the trip!

About the Author

Anne Damrosch was born on Earth Day, and raised in New York City and the Berkshires. After working as a pediatric nurse in Deschapelles, Haiti, in the '80s, she migrated to Vermont where she worked in the field of play therapy with children and families. Throughout, poetry has been a shining thread weaving together her love of children, animals, home and garden, and all things green and growing on our astounding planet.

The body text of poet Anne Damrosch's collection Post & Line is set in Baskerville, a serif typeface designed in the 1750s by John Baskerville, a breakthrough designer of typefaces, influenced by the calligraphy he had learned and taught as a young man, and driven by his passion for bookmaking excellence. As Baskerville said, "Having been an early admirer of the beauty of letters, I became insensibly desirous of contributing to their perfection." John Baskerville developed his own original methods, creating beautifully bright woven paper, darker inks, and higher standards for presses, bringing typography into the modern age. Baskerville's design is a bridge between eras: classically dignified and elegant but modern and stylish; its clean, delicate lines mirror and telegraph the clarity and refined beauty in Damrosch's poetry.

The titles herein are set in Myriad Pro Light, one of the many warm and generously proportioned fonts developed by graphic designer and multimedia artist Carol Twombly in collaboration with Robert Slimbach. Myriad Pro's open shapes lend the titles a tenderness echoed in the poems. Of her designs, Twombly said, "I discovered that...placing black shapes on a white page offered a welcome balance between freedom and structure." Wild Rising Press is proud to present Damrosch's *Post & Line*, poems that succeed brilliantly in that balance—lyrical beauty and crafted modern Voice.